CENGAGE Learning·

Novels for Students, Volume 43

Project Editor: Sara Constantakis Rights Acquisition and Management: Robyn Young Composition: Evi Abou-El-Seoud Manufacturing: Rhonda Dover

Imaging: John Watkins

Product Design: Pamela A. E. Galbreath, Jennifer Wahi Digital Content Production: Allie Semperger Product Manager: Meggin Condino © 2013 Gale, Cengage Learning

For product information and technology assistance, contact us at **Gale Customer Support, 1-800-877-4253.**

For permission to use material from this text or product, submit all requests online at **www.cengage.com/permissions**.

Further permissions questions can be emailed to **permissionrequest@cengage.com** While every effort has been made to ensure the reliability of the information presented in this publication, Gale, a part of Cengage Learning, does not guarantee the accuracy of the data contained herein. Gale accepts no payment for listing; and inclusion in the publication of any organization, agency, institution, publication, service, or individual does not imply endorsement of the editors or publisher. Errors brought to the attention of the publisher and verified to the satisfaction of the publisher will be corrected in future editions.

Gale
27500 Drake Rd.
Farmington Hills, MI, 48331-3535

ISBN-13: 978-1-4144-9486-9
ISBN-10: 1-4144-9486-6
ISSN 1094-3552

This title is also available as an e-book.

ISBN-13: 978-1-4144-9272-8
ISBN-10: 1-4144-9272-3
Contact your Gale, a part of Cengage Learning sales
representative for ordering information.

Printed in Mexico
1 2 3 4 5 6 7 17 16 15 14 13

The Sound of Waves

Yukio Mishima

1954

INTRODUCTION

Yukio Mishima, a Japanese author, actor, director, model, and socialite, stunned the world when, in 1970, at the age of forty-five, he committed ritual suicide in the manner of a samurai warrior after attempting a coup at the headquarters of the Japanese Self-Defense Forces in Tokyo. For this shocking act of seppuku (known in the West by the informal title *hara-kiri*) he became internationally known, but before 1970 he was already an enormous celebrity at home as one of Japan's most talented and prolific writers, admired for his deeply passionate and often violent prose. *The Sound of Waves,* published in 1954, tells a beautiful love story between two island teenagers. Atypical of Mishima's work, the novel is an innocent and subdued retelling of the ancient Greek story of Daphnis and Chloe. Written in Mishima's characteristically sensual style, *The Sound of Waves* was an instant best seller in Japan and received excellent reviews in the United States as the first of his work to be translated into English. Mishima himself was surprised to have produced such an appealing story, calling it, according to John Nathan in *Mishima: A Biography,* "that joke on the public." Despite his affectation of nonchalance, *The Sound of Waves* reflects Mishima's love of Greek culture and history after first visiting the country in 1952. In Greece, the always troubled Mishima learned, as quoted by Nathan, that "creating a beautiful work of art and becoming beautiful oneself were ethically identical." *The Sound of Waves* is the result of this revelation, a glittering outlier in the otherwise dark world of Mishima's fiction. Meredith Weatherby's 1956 translation was republished by Vintage International in 1994.

AUTHOR BIOGRAPHY

Mishima, born in Tokyo, Japan, on January 14, 1925, as Kimitake Hiraoka, was taken to live with his ailing grandmother until he turned twelve. Victims of his grandmother's possessiveness, his father and mother, who lived separately in the same house, were powerless to interfere with her wishes owing to the strict family dynamics of respect. Mishima's two younger siblings lived relatively normal childhoods with their parents, but Mishima, confined to the dark of the apartment downstairs and rarely allowed outside, could only entertain himself quietly with origami, reading, and writing or playing with his female cousins. Released from his grandmother's grasp in 1937, Mishima excelled as a student. He was awarded a silver watch from the emperor as the best student in his high school when he graduated in 1944. During World War II, he escaped the draft as the result of his unhealthy appearance (mistakenly ascribed to tuberculosis). But witnessing the war's devastation on the home front had a profound effect on Mishima, and afterward he never grew accustomed to peace.

Completing law school at Tokyo Imperial University in 1947, Mishima took a highranking bureaucratic position in the Finance Ministry, as was expected of him by his demanding father, who raided his bedroom weekly and destroyed any writing he found. But Kimitake Hiraoka, who had published work under his pseudonym, Yukio

Mishima, since high school, could not continue as a bureaucrat. He quit his job in 1948 to become a novelist. With the publication of his novel *Confessions of a Mask* in 1949, Mishima began his rise to fame. He traveled the world in 1951, stopping in the United States, Brazil, France, and, finally, Greece. His obsession with Greece led to his emulation of Greek classicism in *The Sound of Waves* as well as his adoption of Greek style in dress and decor. When he published *The Sound of Waves* in 1954, the novel broke postwar sales records. By 1956, Mishima was at the height of his fame.

In the mid-1950s, Mishima began bodybuilding, modeling, and acting in films—in an effort to erase his weak appearance, brought on by a childhood spent indoors. He wrote with exceptional self-discipline, usually through the night. In 1958, he married Yoko Sugiyama, and the couple later had two children. In the 1960s, amid antigovernment protests, Mishima turned to radicalism. He gathered a personal army composed mainly of students, called the Shield Society, who were pledged to defend the emperor against the democracy of postwar Japan. He published political essays denouncing outside influence and modernization. His lifelong obsession with death— a product of his disturbing childhood and coming of age in the midst of the destruction of World War II —culminated in a failed coup. Mishima and select men from the Shield Society invaded the headquarters of the Japan Self-Defense Forces in November of 1970, taking the commandant hostage and assembling the soldiers for a speech. Mishima's speech could not be heard over the dissenting crowd. He then knelt in the office of his hostage and drove a sword through his stomach. One of his men then completed the ritual by beheading him. Nathan writes, "In two months, Mishima would have been forty-six. He had written forty novels, eighteen plays (all lavishly performed), twenty volumes of short stories, and as many of literary essays."

PLOT SUMMARY

Chapter 1

The Sound of Waves begins with a description of Uta-jima, or "Song Island"—a small island with magnificent views of the sea. The best views are from the Yashiro Shrine, dedicated to the sea god that the islanders worship, and from the lighthouse, which stands high on a cliff.

After sunset, an eighteen-year-old boy walks the steep path to the lighthouse carrying a fish. He thinks of earlier in the day, as he and the other fishermen were pulling ashore. On the beach he saw a mysterious girl, though she was dressed like a local. The boy passed by close to her, staring into her face. The girl did not shift her gaze from the sea. At first he was happy to have looked but now realizes how rude he was to have stared so openly.

The lighthouse keeper and his wife helped the boy graduate despite flunking his final exams. In gratitude, the boy brings them part of his catch. The wife greets the boy as Shinji and invites him in for dinner.

Chapter 2

At sea, Shinji remembers the night before. He returned from the lighthouse to his home, where his twelve-year-old brother, Hiroshi, and widowed mother live. After dinner, the brothers went to the public bath. Shinji strained to hear gossip of the girl but heard nothing.

On the boat with his master, Jukichi, and his master's apprentice, Ryuji, Shinji distracts himself fishing for octopus. When the men break for lunch, Jukichi mentions the girl—she is the daughter of the wealthy Uncle Teru, who recently lost his wife and only son. Lonely, Uncle Teru brought her back from her adopted family to be married on the island. Shinji realizes with disappointment that he is too poor to be chosen as a husband for the girl, Hatsue. Uncle Teru owns two freighters and is an intimidating man of great esteem on Uta-jima, while Shinji's only wish is to own a single engine-powered boat one day.

Chapter 3

At a meeting of the Young Men's Association, Shinji hears talk of Hatsue. The leader, Yasuo, arrives, son of an important family in the village. He hurries through the meeting, then leaves to attend a party thrown by Uncle Teru for Hatsue's return. Upset, Shinji walks the beach alone, making his way to the Yashiro Shrine, where he tosses two coins in offering. He prays for the safety of his family, success in fishing, and to marry a girl like Hatsue. As he finishes his prayer, the wind picks up. Shinji hopes the sea god accepts his prayer and does not punish him for selfishness.

Chapter 4

In stormy weather, Shinji's mother asks him to collect the firewood she has gathered and stored near an abandoned military tower—the highest point on the island. Inside the tower he finds his mother's firewood but hears someone sobbing. He climbs onto the roof to find Hatsue. She got lost on her way to the lighthouse for etiquette lessons from the lighthouse keeper's wife. Shinji offers to guide her back. As they walk down the slope, Shinji asks Hatsue not to tell anyone they have met: "Thus their well-founded fear of the village's love of gossip changed what was an innocent meeting into a thing of secrecy."

Chapter 5

Shinji overhears gossip that Hatsue is to marry Yasuo. His spirits drop, but he distracts himself fishing. When the fishermen dock, Shinji receives his split of the profit for the week. Shinji stays on the beach to help other boats land. Hatsue is pushing a boat in, but they do not speak. He returns home to give his money to his mother but finds that he has lost his envelope. He runs out of the house to search for it.

Hatsue arrives at the house, returning the envelope she has found to Shinji's mother. She goes out to find Shinji and ease his panic, discovering him on the beach. He asks about the rumor he heard about Yasuo. She denies it. Laughing, she falls to the ground, and Shinji follows her, "Their dry, chapped lips touched. There was a slight taste of salt." They agree to meet at the lighthouse the next day.

Chapter 6

Shinji returns to the Yashiro Shrine to offer a prayer of thanks. The lighthouse couple have grown fond of Hatsue. Their daughter attends college in Tokyo, but they think of the island girls as their own. Shinji arrives for dinner. When the lighthouse keeper's wife sees Shinji and Hatsue smiling shyly at each other, she brings up her daughter Chiyoko's crush on Shinji, who leaves the house abruptly.

MEDIA ADAPTATIONS

- A five-hour audiobook edition of *The Sound of Waves was* released in 2010, with Brian Nishii narrating.

Shinji waits outside, but Hatsue walks right past him. Shinji catches up with her after she trips, dropping her flashlight. She asks about Chiyoko, but Shinji reassures her. They make plans to meet at the abandoned military observation tower the next time a storm hits.

Chapter 7

Hiroshi embarks on a school trip to mainland Japan. The schoolboys travel by ferry and are seen off by their worried mothers. Raised in island isolation, many of the boys are seeing city life for the first time on this trip. After dropping off the children, the ferry returns with Chiyoko, home for spring break, and Yasuo, coming home after a business meeting. Yasuo engages the gloomy Chiyoko in conversation, showing off to the college-educated girl. Chiyoko dislikes Yasuo's arrogance. He helps her onto the boat, but she imagines it is Shinji's hand holding her own. Yasuo mentions Hatsue, her beauty, and his expectation to become her fiancé. Chiyoko is jealous of any mention of beauty, as if it condemns her own plain looks. The boat pulls into harbor at Uta-jima, tilting in the choppy water.

Chapter 8

A storm hits the island. Shinji cannot wait to meet Hatsue. His mother watches in wonder as he sings and jumps around the house, finally going out into the storm. At the beach, Shinji finds a beautiful pink shell before returning home.

After lunch, Shinji takes the path past the lighthouse to the tower. He arrives soaked. Building a fire, he falls asleep in the warm shelter. He wakes to find Hatsue, naked, drying her clothes by the fire. She catches him looking, ordering him to close his eyes. The women of the island dive naked for pearls, so Shinji cannot understand why Hatsue would be uncomfortable. He asks her what would make her comfortable, and she responds that she would be more comfortable if Shinji were naked too. He complies. Just then the storm grows fierce outside, and Shinji leaps over the fire to calm Hatsue. They embrace and lay down on the floor, but Hatsue objects. She wants to marry Shinji but cannot go any further until then. Shinji does not share her views but respects her wishes. He gives her the pink shell. On the way home, they do not separate before the lighthouse as usual but continue on together as the storm whips the island.

Chiyoko has been bored at the lighthouse, the only excitement coming from a meeting of the etiquette class in which she saw and confirmed Hatsue's beauty. Studying at home during the storm, Chiyoko gazes out the lighthouse window, longing for her big-city life in Tokyo. She spots Hatsue and Shinji walking in the rain, holding each other.

Chapter 9

Chiyoko visits Yasuo to tell him what she saw during the storm. Yasuo's sense of entitlement is

deeply injured: "The most unbearable thought of all
—was that Shinji had had his way with the girl
fairly and squarely, with complete honesty." He
studies the schedule of water drawing from the
village well to find the time of Hatsue's turn and
ambushes her that night. He tells her she has slept
with Shinji. She denies it. He attempts to rape her,
but an angry hornet stings him. She escapes. Yasuo
begs her not to tell her father, finally securing her
promise by offering to carry her water jugs back for
her. She follows him at a distance.

Chapter 10

Hiroshi returns from his trip excited beyond
words. But when he and his friends explore an
island cave, he learns of a nasty rumor that his
brother and Hatsue had *omeko*, or slept together. He
asks his mother about it, enraging her. His mother,
embarrassed, asks Shinji if the rumor is true. Shinji
says no, and his mother believes him. Still, the
rumor spreads quickly through the village until
Hatsue's father overhears it in the bathhouse. He
erupts in a rage.

Chapter 11

On the fishing boat, Jukichi hands Shinji a
message from Hatsue. She has been forbidden by
her father to see Shinji, but she will hide notes for
him beneath a water jar outside her house. Jukichi
reads the letter out loud. He and Ryuji feel
sympathetic. Ryuji agrees to retrieve the messages.

The men read the letters daily on the boat. Hatsue writes of Yasuo's attempt to rape her and her father's ambivalence at this news. Meanwhile, Chiyoko learns through gossip that Shinji and Hatsue are forbidden contact. She is overcome with guilt. She goes to Shinji to confess but instead asks him if she is ugly. Shinji answers simply that she is pretty. Delighted, Chiyoko returns to Tokyo for school without confessing.

Chapter 12

Shinji's mother dreams of solving her son's sadness. She goes to Uncle Teru's house, but he will not see her—forcing Hatsue to send her away. Shinji's mother does not tell her son about her failure, but Shinji finds out from Hatsue's letters. They attempt to meet again the night of a party at Uncle Teru's house, but he catches them and calls Hatsue away.

Chapter 13

With the arrival of summer, the women of the island begin pearl-diving season. During a moment of relaxation after a dive, an old peddler interrupts them to show his wares. After a few women make purchases, he suggests an abalone-diving contest, with one of his fashionable purses as a prize. Shinji's mother places second in the contest to gather the most abalone, and Hatsue places first. She gives the prize to Shinji's mother, winning her favor and her forgiveness for turning her away from

Uncle Teru's house.

Chapter 14

One of Uncle Teru's freighters docks at Uta-jima. Yasuo and Shinji are asked to join the crew. Hatsue sneaks Shinji a package with her portrait the day he sets sail. Shinji works hard as a deckhand while Yasuo acts lazy and privileged, quickly falling out of favor with the captain. A strong typhoon approaches, endangering the freighter at its port in Okinawa. A cable anchoring the ship snaps suddenly in the powerful wind. Shinji volunteers to swim out to the buoy to reattach the broken cable. He barely survives the dangerous waves and harsh wind but completes his task, saving freighter and crew.

Chapter 15

Returning to Uta-jima, Shinji gives thanks at Yashiro Shrine and celebrates his homecoming at Jukichi's house. Chiyoko admits her guilt to her mother in a letter, refusing to return to the island until her mother persuades Uncle Teru to allow Shinji and Hatsue to be together. The lighthouse keeper's wife respects her daughter's wish, enlisting other women of the village to help her convince Uncle Teru that Shinji is worthy. They crowd into his house, only to discover that Uncle Teru has changed his mind after hearing of Shinji's heroic actions during the typhoon.

Chapter 16

Shinji and Hatsue walk up the many steps to Yashiro Shrine to announce their engagement and give thanks to the sea god. Next, they go to the lighthouse to have dinner with the couple. Shinji has no idea of Chiyoko's role in the drama that has just unfolded. The lighthouse keeper takes them up the stairs to the lighthouse itself, tactfully leaving them alone. They gaze out at the beautiful view of the ocean. Hatsue shows Shinji the pink shell he gave her, and Shinji takes out the picture Hatsue gave him. Shinji realizes it was not the picture of Hatsue but "his own strength that had tided him through that perilous night."

Chiyoko

Chiyoko is the serious-minded daughter of the lighthouse keepers. She has an unrequited crush on Shinji. Yasuo tries to impress her as she takes the ferry back to Uta-jima for spring break from her college in Tokyo. But Chiyoko is not impressed: "She was always wishing that she could have a man look at her at least once with eyes saying 'I love you' instead of 'You love me.'" At home, she catches Shinji and Hatsue walking to the village together in the storm and, jealous, tells Yasuo— starting the rumor that Shinji and Hatsue slept together. When she finds out that this has caused the two to be separated, she feels guilty and regretful. After Shinji tells her that she is pretty during a confrontation on the beach, she returns to Tokyo for school. She refuses to come back to Uta-jima until Shinji and Hatsue are together, asking her mother in a letter to act as the go-between in their engagement. Although she likes Shinji, he is in the dark about Chiyoko's deep feelings and rash actions in the novel.

Hatsue

Hatsue is the daughter of Uncle Teru. She was adopted away at an early age, but after the deaths of his wife and only son, Uncle Teru brings Hatsue back to the island to live with him. She has a rustic beauty, attracting both Shinji and Yasuo. However, she loves Shinji and detests Yasuo after he attempts to rape her. Hatsue is well mannered, earning the admiration of the lighthouse couple. She is intelligent and respectful of island morals, except when her father bans her from seeing Shinji. After Uncle Teru makes Hatsue ask Shinji's mother to leave the house, she apologizes by winning a purse for his mother in the abalone-diving contest: "The mother's simple, straightforward heart had immediately understood the modesty and respect behind the girl's gesture." She gives Shinji a portrait of herself to take with him on the freighter. When he returns safely, they are engaged to be married.

Hiroshi

Hiroshi is Shinji's twelve-year-old brother. Shinji and his mother support his education through fishing and pearl diving, respectively. Hiroshi is beside himself with excitement for his first trip by ferry to the mainland. He sends home a postcard about seeing his first movie that reduces his mother to proud tears. When he returns to Uta-jima, he cannot put his feelings into words. Instead, he remembers a prank he once pulled: polishing a spot on the floor at school so thoroughly that a teacher slipped and fell. That is all he can think of when he remembers the flashing streetcars and tangle of lights and metal that was the mainland. He returns to his normal island life, playing with his friends from school. He learns from them the rumor that

Shinji and Hatsue slept together and repeats this rumor to his mother.

Jukichi

Jukichi is a master fisherman with two apprentices on his fishing boat, Shinji and Ryuji. When Shinji's luck in love runs out, Jukichi is moved by sympathy. He reads Hatsue's letters aloud on the boat each day during lunch and gives excellent advice to the unfortunate Shinji, such as to not physically attack Yasuo after he learns of the attempted rape. Jukichi is asked to release Shinji from his boat temporarily to work on Uncle Teru's freighter. He realizes Shinji is being tested for Hatsue's hand in marriage. He is very proud of Shinji's actions during the typhoon, and the two get drunk on sake, celebrating his safe return to Uta-jima.

Lighthouse Keeper

The lighthouse keeper is a former serviceman who now works in the lighthouse, charting the paths of ships and telegraphing locations to ports. He is a kindly man who cares for Shinji and Hatsue. When the two are finally engaged, he takes them on a tour of the lighthouse, leaving them alone at the very top.

Lighthouse Keeper's Wife

The lighthouse keeper's wife, or mistress of the

lighthouse, conducts etiquette lessons with the village girls. She is an avid reader of celebrity magazines and has a love for learning. Her only daughter, Chiyoko, goes to college in Tokyo, but she and her husband care for all of the children in the village. They adore Shinji, who is indebted to them for helping him finish high school. However, the lighthouse keeper's wife upsets Shinji, Hatsue, and her husband when she mentions Chiyoko's feelings for Shinji at an inappropriate moment. However, her intentions are usually good. After her daughter refuses to come home out of guilt, the lighthouse keeper's wife marches right into Uncle Teru's house to argue on Shinji and Hatsue's behalf.

Old Peddler

The old peddler comes to Uta-jima to sell his wares to the women of the island. He finds them recovering their strength by a fire after diving for pearls. He organizes a playful contest in which the woman who collects the most abalone will win one of three purses. One purse is for a younger woman, one is fashionable for a middle-aged woman, and one purse suits a distinguished older woman. When Hatsue wins the contest, she picks the purse most appealing for a middle-aged woman and presents it to Shinji's mother.

Ryuji

Ryuji is an apprentice of Jukichi's on the fishing boat. He is younger than Shinji but sympathetic to his troubles with Hatsue. He volunteers to act as messenger for the couple, hiding and retrieving messages hidden under a water jar on Uncle Teru's property.

Shinji

Shinji is the hero of *The Sound of Waves*: levelheaded, strong, and pure of heart. He works as a fisherman on Jukichi's boat to help support his family. He brings fish to the lighthouse couple to show his appreciation for their help in his graduation from school. He prays to the sea god at Yashiro Shrine, giving yen (Japanese currency) in offering despite his poverty. He and Hatsue share a deep love for each other that they are too young to fully express. However, Shinji does all he can to be with Hatsue and never lets hope die in his heart. He joins the crew of Uncle Teru's ship, saving it from destruction in a typhoon and proving himself worthy of Hatsue. Shinji is associated with natural and spiritual forces in the island throughout the novel: "He heard the sound of waves striking the shore, and it was as though the surging of his young blood was keeping time with the movement of the sea's great tides." But Shinji comes to realize at the end that it was his strength alone that carried him through the storm safely.

Shinji's Mother

Shinji's mother is widowed, with two sons: Shinji and Hiroshi. She supports her family by diving for pearls. Her husband died during the war, when a plane bombed his rescue boat. She cries at the thought that her sons will leave the island one day, though she feels that it is inevitable. When Hiroshi is on his school trip and Shinji leaves the house during the storm, she sits alone in the house admiring her own body, which is smooth and fit from pearl-diving. She boasts to herself that she could have five more children with such an attractive body and then, ashamed, prays before her husband's shrine. When Uncle Teru turns her away from his house, she does not tell Shinji because of her embarrassment. After Hatsue apologizes for this incident by giving Shinji's mother a purse, Shinji's mother approves of Hatsue and hopes for the couple to be together.

Uncle Teru

Uncle Teru is a wealthy islander who owns two freighters. His daughter, Hatsue, is his youngest, unmarried child. He lost his wife and only son, causing him great loneliness. He then brought Hatsue home from her adopted family to cure this loneliness. He wants to find a worthy husband for his daughter. At first, it seems that this will be Yasuo. Shinji is too poor to even be considered at first, and after the rumor that Hatsue and Shinji have slept together reaches Uncle Teru, he bans them from seeing each other. But when Shinji proves himself after Uncle Teru tests his character (through working on the freighter), Uncle Teru gives in to his daughter's wishes and allows them to be engaged. He also plans to support Shinji's struggling family by taking them in.

Yasuo

Yasuo is the leader of the Young Men's Association. A wealthy teen from a prominent family on the island, he feels that he is perfect to be chosen as Hatsue's husband. When Chiyoko tells him what she saw the day of the storm, he becomes enraged and hides in the bushes by the well, waiting for Hatsue. He attacks Hatsue and tries to rape her. A hornet, disturbed by his movement in the bushes, stings him all over his body, preventing the rape: "Yasuo would have liked to run away without more ceremony, but his fear that she would tell her father kept him wheedling." He begs her not to tell Teru, promising to carry her water home for her. Hatsue allows him to carry the water but tells her father about the attempt anyway. He and Shinji are chosen to join the crew of Uncle Teru's freighter, where Yasuo proves himself to be lazy. The captain grows to dislike him. Yasuo loses favor with Uncle Teru as a result of his selfish, privileged behavior on the freighter.

THEMES

Love

At the heart of *The Sound of* Waves is the love story between Hatsue and Shinji, reminiscent of a fairy-tale romance in its structure. The two young lovers are at odds with the world because Shinji's poverty makes him ineligible as a suitor for the daughter of the wealthiest islander. But fate intervenes, and the two meet on the roof of the observation tower, unobserved. Their actions together are harmonious, yet secretive. Although they respect the moral code of the island, their private meetings stir vicious rumors. Still, the couple remains independent of others' wishes, passing notes and pursuing their love under the radar of Uncle Teru. Chiyoko's jealousy and Yasuo's fiendish plan are trumped. First Shinji's mother, then the lighthouse keepers, and finally stubborn Uncle Teru are won to the lovers' side. They stay loyal to their own wishes and are rewarded for this strength of will, but they pay tribute to those who helped them come together: a purse for Shinji's mother, a prayer at Yashiro Shrine, and dinner at the lighthouse each announce the couple as a legitimate and respectful new addition to the insular culture of Uta-jima.

Rites of Passage

Shinji faces many tests on Uta-jima. He must brave storms, rough seas, temptation, and deceitful gossip. However, his strong, honest actions in the end prove his worth. When Chiyoko tests him on the beach, asking suddenly if she is pretty, Shinji's affirmative response is a pure one: "As everyone well knew, Shinji was incapable of flattery." Because his honest answer delights Chiyoko, she eventually asks her mother to help him find happiness with Hatsue. But the greatest challenge comes on Uncle Teru's freighter, when a cable snaps in the winds of the typhoon. Shinji's feat of courage and strength in the water saves Uncle Teru's property and crew: "The boy swam with all his might. And, inch by inch, step by step, the huge mass of the enemy fell back, opening the way for him." By surviving this trial at sea, Shinji becomes a man worthy of Hatsue.

TOPICS FOR FURTHER STUDY

- Form groups of two or three and scan the novel for instances of symbolism. Using your memory of the book, as well as the help of flipping through the text, try as a group to discover a few symbols as well as what you think each symbol represents. Write down what you find as a group to prepare for class discussion.

- Mishima is one of the most translated Japanese authors of his time. Read another work by Mishima and then write a comparative essay in which you discuss the opinion that *The Sound of Waves* represents an exception to Mishima's usual style. How do the two works compare in language, content, setting, protagonists, or any other aspect you find important? Which work do you prefer?

- Write a short story or poem based on your favorite myth or fairy tale. Be creative as you reimagine the story. Your work can be any length, but be sure to note which story you chose to retell. For a guide to common myths, reference *Aesop's Fables: A Classic Illustrated Edition*, published by Chronicle Books in 1990 or *D'Aulaires' Book of Greek*

Myths, published by Delacorte Books for Young Readers in 1992.

- Read a work by another Japanese author of your choice. What conclusions can you draw about Japanese fiction using Mishima and your chosen author as examples? Consider aspects of style, form, and content. Write an essay with quotes from the books to support your examples. Some Japanese authors to consider are Haruki Murakami, Yasunari Kawabata, Junichiro Tanizaki, Akira Yoshimura, Kenzaburo Oe, Kobo Abe, and Yoko Ogawa.

- Mishima based Uta-jima on a real island. Using your online search skills, discover the name of the island. Compile information about that island, which could include its population, a map or picture of the island, its nearby neighbors, or anything else that you found interesting during your search. Hint: Although there is a real island named Uta-jima, this is not the correct answer.

Although Shinji is the hero of this tale, he is not the only character who must complete a rite of passage in the novel. Hatsue must prove her worth to Shinji's mother after a disastrous meeting between the two at Uncle Teru's house. Both women work in the dangerous depths of the sea as pearl divers and compete against each other in the old peddler's abalone-diving contest. Yet when Hatsue wins, she gives the prize to Shinji's mother, apologizing respectfully for her earlier actions at her father's house: "Hatsue smiled, and Shinji's mother told herself how wise her son had been in his choice of a bride.... And it was in this same fashion that the politics of the island were always conducted." Typical of Hatsue's demure personality, she works within the moral code of the island to accomplish her goal of a life with Shinji.

Although he is younger than the hero and heroine, Hiroshi experiences a rite of passage as well. He is of age to journey to the mainland for the first time. Stunned by the contrast between Uta-jima and the modern metropolis, he can find no words to describe it when he returns home: "Those towering buildings and neon lights that had so amazed him— where were they now?" By nightfall on the day of his return Hiroshi has, like those who made the trip before him, resettled into his rural life: "At the end of long lives spent on the island they would no longer even so much as remember the ... streetcars clanging back and forth along the streets of a city."

Self-reliance

Shinji and the other villagers of Uta-jima are

characterized as strong, healthy, and independent. The islanders may not have wealth, but they can support themselves. Self-reliant people such as Jukichi, Shinji's fishing master; the lighthouse couple; and Shinji's mother, whose skin is unwrinkled by age, populate the book as positive forces. Meanwhile, Yasuo, a product of his parents' money, acts lazy and entitled throughout the novel, serving as the villain. Self-reliance, as opposed to Yasuo's selfishness, means helping others, as well as oneself, succeed, and many characters are seen at the aid of their fellow villagers—culminating in the gang of women who storm Uncle Teru's house to demand Shinji and Hatsue be allowed to love each other. Although the sea god is placated with prayers and Hatsue's love comes at the end with the support of the villagers, who abandon their gossiping in favor of approval, Shinji realizes in the surprising final line that he is singularly responsible for surviving the typhoon and thus in control of his own destiny.

STYLE

Pastoral

In retelling Longus's *Daphnis and Chloe*, an ancient Greek pastoral, Richard F. Hardin writes in *Love in a Green Shade*: "Mishima removes the setting from the world of shepherds to that of rural types more familiar to his readers, fishermen." The setting, or the outside world surrounding and influencing the characters, plays a significant role in *The Sound of Waves*. Uta-jima, a small, self-reliant, and picturesque island, provides the fantasy-like backdrop to the romance of Hatsue and Shinji. Pastoral works, so called for their pasture setting describing the pleasant, simple rural life, have existed as long as storytelling, but Mishima reengineers this common genre in Japanese terms. Gwenn Boardman Petersen writes in *The Moon in the Water*, "The sea and sky, the scents and sounds of the enchanted island, are beautifully evoked in language reminiscent of the harmony of old Japan." The Yashiro Shrine is the spiritual center of the book and one of the highest physical points on the island, where prayers to the sea god are earnestly whispered and hard-earned money given up in offering. The village generator is broken, bathing the island in darkness, and the pearl-diving women work unself-consciously in the nude. These aspects of life cannot be found in the big city, and Hardin points out how Hiroshi's school trip "allows the usual country-city contrast." Returning home to Uta-jima after his surreal trip to the mainland, "his became again an existence in which everything was understood without the need for words." By surrounding Hatsue and Shinji's drama with such a setting, in which life is tranquil and complications are few, Mishima's love story is made more powerful as trouble comes to the little island.

Folklore

Mishima uses folklore to lend his love story on Uta-jima a deeper history and significance. Folklore —the stories and beliefs of a culture passed down orally through generations—unites the island characters as members of the same culture with shared cultural knowledge. Their superstitions, legends, and stories illustrate their specific outlook on life. For example, when a woman who dives too deeply off the shore falls ill and dies, the other pearl divers say that it is because she saw something in the depths that humans were not supposed to see. This story—that humans will be punished by the divine for reaching too far into the unknown— illustrates the conservative nature of the islanders, a conservatism Shinji and Hatsue must defeat when their love for each other is not accepted as appropriate. On their side is Shinji's mother, who dived even deeper after the woman died, clearly a more daring woman than the other divers and willing to break the rules.

In another tale from the island's folklore, a

wealthy royal named Prince Deki floated to the island on a golden ship, took a local girl as his wife, and lived out his years on Uta-jima peacefully. The legend of Prince Deki inspires both Shinji and Hatsue (who each have a dream about the prince) to persevere against their troubles. Like Prince Deki, Shinji feels that he is destined to live peacefully on Uta-jima with Hatsue by his side. As the tragic story of the diver teaches a lesson in conservatism, Prince Deki, a mythical figure on the island, illustrates the islanders' feelings about their small home. Uta-jima is fit for a prince—even a prince who sails in a golden ship. The legend of Prince Deki idealizes the islanders' lives of peaceful isolation. Uta-jima's folklore adds an additional layer of meaning to Shinji and Hatsue's story as deep-rooted cultural beliefs both aid and hinder the lovers.

HISTORICAL CONTEXT

Postwar Japan

Mishima was a member of Japan's war generation. Jan Walsh Hokenson writes in *Japan, France, and East-West Aesthetics*: "He had survived the war, as a boy in Tokyo, under American bombings then occupation. He saw the profound Westernization of the country during 1950 to 1965." The war never left him. Coming of age in the midst of destruction and terror, Mishima could not reconcile the later peaceful years with what he had seen as a young man. Even in isolated Uta-jima, the war has made its mark. Hatsue and Shinji meet in an abandoned military observation tower, now used by the villagers to store their firewood. In the otherwise tranquil novel's most graphic scene, Mishima reveals how Shinji's father died: "The plane dropped a bomb on the boat and then strafed it with machine-gun fire.... Both the deck and the bilge became a lake of blood."

After surrendering, Japan came under the occupation of American forces under General Douglas MacArthur, and for the first time the country was exposed to outside influence. Hiroshi, on a trip to the mainland of Japan, sends home a telling postcard of Westernization's hypnotizing effect: "Hiroshi's closely written card was all about seeing his first motion picture, with not so much as a word about the famous scenic spots and historic places he was seeing." Uta-jima suffered in the war, but the effects of Westernization have not spread to the island. This is Mishima's ideal, for he grew more extreme with time toward the loss of Japanese tradition as the result of the popularization of Western ways. One exception Mishima allowed was for Greece, as Gwen Boardmaan Petersen explains: "Mishima worshipped at the Greek temple while urging, right up to the moment of his *seppuku*, a revival of the Japanese spirit."

Greek Influence

In 1952, when he was already a celebrity in Japan, Mishima traveled to Greece on the last leg of a vacation around the globe. A friend had given Mishima press credentials from his magazine so that he could leave the country for the first time. As Nathan notes, in postwar Japan "there were still no passports, only travel permits signed by MacArthur himself, and these were next to impossible to get." Mishima went to San Francisco, New York, Rio de Janeiro, and Paris, but Greece was his ultimate destination.

In Athens, the beauty and history of the ruins of ancient Greek civilization affected Mishima deeply. He wrote, as Nathan quotes, "Greece cured my self-hatred and my loneliness and awoke in me a *will to health*." Back home in Tokyo he enrolled in a Greek language course and began to mimic Greek fashion. But the most sophisticated expression of

Mishima's love of Greece and the happiness he found pursuing this love is *The Sound of Waves*, written in 1954 at the peak of his passion. The novel's ideal setting and heroic characters follow the original *Daphnis and Chloe* closely. Petersen writes, "Mishima's island … blend[s] elements of universal fairy tale, of the Greek hero-against-the-sea, and of a Japanese past of gods."

Shinji and Hatsue's trials to prove their love, the chorus of gossiping villagers, and the ageless physical fitness of the pearl divers and fishermen reflect Greek traditions as Mishima saw them with an innocence not found in his other work. Shinji stands "like some piece of heroic sculpture," and with his body "shining in the flames" he leaps over a fire to comfort Hatsue. A year after *The Sound of Waves* was published. Mishima began weight lifting in order to achieve the same heroic physique. Petersen writes, "Physical perfection is in his view linked to Greek wisdom." He had observed this perfection in Greek statues, and he had written about it in the character of Shinji—the simple but valiant hero who combines the best of Greek and Japanese virtues.

COMPARE & CONTRAST

- **1954:** After the end of World War II, modernization and Westernization begin to spread across the defeated country, rapidly overtaking older traditions of

Japanese society.

Today: Emerging from loss as a world power, Japan has become respected for great modernizing achievements across many fields, including technology, entertainment, and business.

- **1954:** Pearl diving is a traditional occupation for the rural women of fishing villages, a physically challenging and dangerous job performed in cold water with no protective gear.

Today: Japan has modernized the collection of pearls through the growing of pearl cultures, making pearls easier to harvest. No longer strictly a job for rural women, pearl collection is a Japanese industry.

- **1954:** Shrines such as the Yashiro Shrine on Uta-jima island are important religious sites to the Japanese people, where offerings of money can be made to the gods in the hope that the supplicant's prayers will be answered.

Today: Shrines are still prominent throughout the country, attracting visitors from around the world to view these beautifully preserved landmarks. Money given in offering is used to protect and repair the shrines for future visitors.

CRITICAL OVERVIEW

The Sound of Waves broke postwar sales records in Japan. In America, Meredith Weatherby's translation of the novel received widespread praise. This was Mishima's first novel to appear in English, chosen to be released before earlier work by Mishima for its more subdued treatment of sexuality. While unanimously acknowledging it as a great novel, literary critics often focus on the mood of *The Sound of Waves* compared with the majority of Mishima's work. Nathan describes *The Sound of Waves* as a "sunlit book" and believes that "the book is unremittingly normal in the most conventional sense; in fact, it is Mishima's most assiduously healthy work." Hokenson states that Mishima "had been known in the West as a novelist of brilliantly somber themes, descriptive skill, lyric power, and an extraordinary breadth of knowledge." That he produced such a compelling love story, free of the shock implicit in his other work, most critics link to his Greece-induced high spirits. Nathan writes of Mishima's determination "to demonstrate to himself not only that he was capable of creating a world so different from his own but even that he had a place in it." Petersen writes of Mishima's reception in his own country, "It is not surprising that Japanese critics—including his mentor Kawabata—use such terms as 'ornate' and 'gorgeous' in describing Mishima's language." Some impressive and untranslatable elements of

Mishima's syntax, such as puns and other plays on words, are lost in the conversion to English. However, his work with color translates perfectly: "Dark whirlpools and stormy waters hint at mystic depths of the past, while foaming water, white freighter and brilliant beams of lighthouse and beacon suggest the hero's conquest ...of a threatening universe." In *Love in a Green Shade*, Hardin states that the novel "offers an affecting and human story reviving the possibility of an authentic idyllicism or joyous unity in love and nature." This is very much in line with the classic Greek text that Mishima is emulating in *The Sound of Waves*. Hardin continues, "Mishima finds a way to put novelistic realism in the service of Greek romance material: scrupulous description and character psychology coexist with sympathizing nature." Patrick M. O'Neil, in *Great World Writers: Twentieth Century*, argues that although the book tells a tranquil story, Mishima's dark tone lives on beneath the surface: "Even in the earliest idyllic fairy-tale romance, *The Sound of Waves*, characters seem happiest when a happy ending is not certain." As examples, he points to the drawn-out process of secret letter writing and the slow walk Shinji takes up the steps of the temple "to meet his beloved Hatsue." These moments of savoring the anticipation, not the actual goal, are capped by the final line of the novel: Shinji realizes—with Hatsue at last by his side—that it was his own power alone that allowed him to survive the storm. This surprising jab at the otherwise mystically unified nature of their love is more the Mishima aesthetic,

as it is known in Japan, than the coming together of
two happy lovers in a peaceful place.

SOURCES

Hardin, Richard F., *Love in a Green Shade: Idyllic Romances Ancient to Modern*, University of Nebraska Press, 2000, pp. 223–24.

Hokenson, Jan Walsh, *Japan, France, and East-West Aesthetics: French Literature, 1867–2000,* Farleigh Dickenson University Press, 2004, p. 316.

Mishima, Yukio, *The Sound of Waves*, translated by Meredith Weatherby, Vintage International, 1994.

Nathan, John, *Mishima: A Biography*, Da Capo Press, 2000, pp. xiv, 110, 115, 120–21.

O'Neil, Patrick M., *Great World Writers: Twentieth Century*, Vol. 7, Marshall Cavendish, 2004, p. 913.

Petersen, Gwenn Boardman, *The Moon in the Water: Understanding Tanizaki, Kawabata, and Mishima*, University of Hawaii Press, 1979, pp. 201, 204–205, 217–19, 221, 252–53, 255.

Spencer, J. E., "Marine Life and Animals in Oriental Economy," in *Asia, East by South: A Cultural Geography*, John Wiley & Sons, 1954, pp. 90–105.

FURTHER READING

Keene, Donald, *Five Modern Japanese Novelists*, Columbia University Press, 2005.

> Keene introduces Western readers to the lives and works of Mishima, Junichiro Tanizaki, Yasunari Kawabata, Kobo Abe, and Ryotaro Shiba in this book of essays that includes reflections on personal encounters with each of these important novelists. Keene is a well-respected scholar of Japanese literature and has a unique perspective on Mishima as one of his closest friends.

Napier, Susan, *Escape from the Wasteland: Romanticism and Realism in the Fiction of Mishima Yukio and Oe Kenzaburo*, Harvard University Asia Center, 1996.

> In *Escape from the Wasteland*, Napier compares the work of Mishima and Oe in the context of postwar Japan. After the war left Japan in ruins, the country was opened to outside influence for the first time in its very long history. Both Mishima's and Oe's works are rife with the effects of this sudden cultural shift, despite their opposing

political and social beliefs.

Ross, Christopher, *Mishima's Sword: Travels in Search of a Samurai Legend*, Da Capo Press, 2006.

> Ross traveled to Japan in search of the antique sword that Mishima had used in his ritual suicide. In *Mishima's Sword*, he tells the story of this journey off the beaten path, exploring unfamiliar cultural territory while discovering more about Mishima's biography and aesthetic.

Yourcenar, Marguerite, *Mishima: A Vision of the Void*, translated by Alberto Manquel, University of Chicago Press, 2001.

> *Mishima: A Vision of the Void* details Mishima's life from birth to death, with a specific focus on Mishima's challenging family life as a child, the enormous effect of Western influence on his behavior and writing style, and his final act of seppuku. Mishima's life is as complex as it is impressive, but a great darkness followed and eventually consumed him. Any biography of Mishima is not for the faint of heart.

SUGGESTED SEARCH TERMS

Yukio Mishima The Sound of Waves

Daphnis and Chloe

Pastoral novel

Postwar

Japan

Japanese shrines

Pearl diving

Greek classicism

Japanese folklore

CPSIA information can be obtained
at www.ICGtesting.com
Printed in the USA
BVHW041038120721
611731BV00016B/701

9 781375 397384